Leverage and Risk

Subtitle:

The Intricate World of Carry Trades in
Global Markets, How the Yen Carry Trade
Shaped Global Economic Policies

BEN WHITE

Copyright ©

Table of Contents

Chapter 1. Introduction   **8**

   What is a Carry Trade?   8

   The Appeal of Carry Trades   10

   Overview of the Book   13

Chapter 2. History and Origins   **17**

   Early Examples of Currency Arbitrage   17

   Evolution of Carry Trades in Financial
   Markets   19

   Major Milestones in Carry Trade History
   21

Chapter 3. Mechanics of Carry Trade   **26**

   Understanding Interest Rate Differentials
   26

   The Role of Currency Volatility   29

   How Carry Trades are Executed   32

Chapter 4. Economic Impact   **35**

   Influence on Global Financial Markets   35

   Effects on National Economies   38

   Case Studies of Economic Impact   42

Chapter 5. Real-Life Examples   **46**

   The Yen Carry Trade   46

The Icelandic Financial Crisis   48

The Role of Emerging Markets   51

Chapter 6. Risk and Reward   55

Potential Gains from Carry Trades   55

Risks Involved in Carry Trades   58

Managing and Mitigating Risks   60

Chapter 7. Carry Trade in Practice   65

Institutional vs. Retail Investors   65

Strategies Employed by Hedge Funds 69

Tools and Platforms for Executing Carry Trades   71

Chapter 8. Myths and Misconceptions 76

Common Misunderstandings about Carry Trades   76

Debunking Popular Myths   79

Realities vs. Perceptions   82

Chapter 9. Popular Beliefs and Cultural Impact   86

The Carry Trade in Financial Media   86

Cultural Perceptions and Misperceptions 89

Carry Trades in Pop Culture   92

Chapter 10. Case Studies   95

Successful Carry Trade Strategies   95

High-Profile Failures   98

Lessons Learned from Past Trades   101

Chapter 11. Regulatory Environment 105

How Governments and Regulators View Carry Trades   105

Major Regulatory Changes Over Time 108

Impact of Regulation on Carry Trade Viability   112

Chapter 12. Future of Carry Trades   116

Emerging Trends and Developments 116

The Role of Technology and AI   120

Predictions for the Future   124

Conclusion   128

Summary of Key Points   128

The Enduring Appeal of Carry Trades 133

Final Thoughts   135

Appendices   138

Glossary of Terms   138

Bibliography and Further Reading   141

Chapter 1. Introduction

- What is a Carry Trade?
- The Appeal of Carry Trades
- Overview of the Book

What is a Carry Trade?

In a carry trade, an investor takes out a low-interest loan in one currency and uses it to make investments in a different currency with a higher interest rate. The idea of profiting from interest rate differences between two countries is the foundation of this business. The objective is to make money from any prospective increase in the value of the investment currency as well as from the discrepancy between the cost of borrowing and the profits on the investment.

It's critical to comprehend the fundamentals of interest rate dynamics and foreign exchange (forex) markets in order to comprehend carry trades. Currency prices vary in forex markets due to a wide range of reasons, such as central bank policies, economic indicators, and geopolitical events. Currencies are exchanged in pairs. Currency values are mostly determined by interest rates, which are established by central banks. A nation's currency usually gains value when interest rates are high because investors are looking for bigger returns. On the other hand, low-interest currencies typically lose value.

The carry trade's mechanics are not too complicated. An investor finds a currency (the funding currency) that has a low interest rate and takes out a loan in that currency. The investor uses the borrowed money to purchase assets denominated in the target currency at the same time as they identify a different currency (the target currency) with a higher interest rate. A carry trade yields a profit from the difference in interest rates as well as any benefits from positive changes in exchange rates. An investor can profit from the interest rate differential, for instance, if they borrow money in Japanese yen, which has historically had low interest rates, and invest it in Australian dollars, which usually have higher interest rates. An increase in value of the Australian dollar relative to the yen benefits the investor.

The Appeal of Carry Trades

For a number of reasons, carry trades have been a well-liked approach among institutional and individual investors alike. The possibility for large gains is one of the main draws. Investors can get returns that are far larger than those of traditional investments in low-interest-rate conditions by taking advantage of the interest rate differential between two currencies. When interest rates are low globally and yield-seeking investors are looking for ways to increase their profits, this is especially alluring.

The simplicity of carry trades is another attraction. The fundamental idea of borrowing money at a low interest rate and investing it at a high rate is simple to comprehend, in contrast to more complicated financial strategies that call for in-depth knowledge and sophisticated technologies. Carry trades are now available to a wide spectrum of investors, from big hedge funds to individual traders, thanks to their ease.

Carry trades can also help with diversification. Adding investments in other currencies can help spread risk and lower overall volatility in a well-constructed portfolio. When the market is choppy and traditional asset classes like stocks and bonds are more volatile, diversification can be very helpful.

Carry trades are appealing for reasons other than their simplicity and high return potential. The approach presents an opportunity for a number of investors to profit from global macroeconomic developments. Interest rate differences emerge as global central banks determine their monetary policies, offering carry trade opportunities. Investors can take advantage of these patterns if they are skilled at interpreting macroeconomic data and forecasting the actions of central banks.

Carry trades are not risk-free, despite these benefits. Currency risk, which results from changes in exchange rates, is the biggest risk. The investor may sustain considerable losses if the borrowed currency gains a substantial value relative to the target currency. Furthermore, carry trades are extremely susceptible to shifts in central banks' interest rate policies. The profitability of the trade may be damaged by an abrupt increase in interest rates by the financing currency's central bank, which might cause a quick unwinding of bets and possible market turbulence.

Overview of the Book

The goal of this book is to give readers a thorough grasp of carry trades by going over their history, workings, and effects on international financial markets. It is designed to walk readers through all the different aspects of this fascinating financial tactic, including information on the advantages and disadvantages of carry trades.

We start by taking a historical look at the beginnings of carry trades and how they have changed over time. It is essential to comprehend the historical background because it illuminates the ways in which carry trades have impacted financial markets and economic policies. We will examine prominent examples of carry trades and their significance in key financial events, including the carry trade of Japanese yen.

We next get into the specifics of carry trade mechanics and give a thorough description of how they operate. Important ideas include interest rate differentials, currency volatility, and the function of central banks will all be covered in this section. We will also look at the methods and resources that investors utilize, including as margin trading, leverage, and risk management plans, to conduct out carry trades.

The book then delves into the macro and microeconomic effects of carry trading. We will examine the ways in which carry trades impact national economies, the global financial markets, and market volatility. Case studies of particular carry trade scenarios will show how they affect real-world situations and provide important insights into their dynamics.

We'll also talk about the misconceptions and fallacies related to carry trades. Despite their widespread use, carry trades are sometimes misinterpreted; this section seeks to dispel common misconceptions and make clear the practical aspects of the approach. We will look at how carry trades are portrayed in the media and financial literature in order to investigate prevailing ideas and cultural impressions of them.

The book contains in-depth case studies of both successful and unsuccessful carry trades to offer a practical viewpoint. These case studies will emphasize the tactics investors used, the difficulties they encountered, and the results of their transactions. Readers can better grasp the subtleties and intricacies of carry trades by taking a lesson from these real-world examples.

Lastly, we explore upcoming trends and advancements in the carry trade industry as we turn our attention to the future. The future of carry trades will be discussed in this section along with how market conditions, regulatory changes, and technological improvements are influencing it. In addition, we will share our knowledge of potential hazards and possibilities that investors should be mindful of when navigating this ever-changing market.

Chapter 2. History and Origins

- Early Examples of Currency Arbitrage
- Evolution of Carry Trades in Financial Markets
- Major Milestones in Carry Trade History

Early Examples of Currency Arbitrage

The technique of taking advantage of pricing disparities between marketplaces, or currency arbitrage, is an old financial tactic that existed before contemporary financial systems. Early instances date back to the Middle Ages, when cross-regional trade was burgeoning and merchants used currency exchange to ease trade. A historical account of currency arbitrage dates back to the Mediterranean region, when traders from

Venice operated triangle trade lines connecting Europe, the Middle East, and Asia. Profiting from variations in exchange rates, they would purchase products in one area using local currency, sell them in another area for a different currency, and then convert the proceeds back into the original currency.

Higher-level currency arbitrage was made possible in the 19th century by the development of global commerce networks and telegraph transmission. Now, traders may take immediate action in response to price disparities in various marketplaces. As major financial centers, London and New York, for instance, saw traders taking advantage of market arbitrage opportunities. Traders would purchase the less expensive currency and sell the more expensive one, locking in a profit without taking any risks, if the exchange rate between the US dollar and the British pound was different from the rate suggested by the price of gold in each market.

Evolution of Carry Trades in Financial Markets

The 20th century saw a substantial evolution in the idea of carry trades as we know it today. Carry trades were initially mostly made by banks and other big financial entities. These organizations realized they could make significant returns by borrowing money in currencies with low interest rates and investing it in assets with higher yields. Such methods developed in a stable environment, which was created by the Bretton Woods Agreement and the creation of fixed exchange rates following World War II.

A crucial turning point in the development of carry trades was the fall of the Bretton

Woods system in the early 1970s, which resulted in the introduction of floating exchange rates. Interest rate differences become more noticeable as a result of currencies being allowed to fluctuate, which increased the chances for carry trades. Traders might now take advantage of the possibility of both interest rate gains and advantageous currency movements by borrowing money in low-interest currencies and investing in assets valued in higher-yielding currencies.

During this time, carry trades involving the Japanese yen were among the first and most well-known. Japan kept interest rates incredibly low as part of its monetary policy to promote economic growth throughout the 1980s and 1990s. Global investors took advantage of the cheap cost of borrowing yen to purchase higher-yielding assets like Australian shares and US Treasury bonds. This era was marked by the yen carry trade, which fueled large capital movements and had an impact on international financial markets.

Major Milestones in Carry Trade History

1. The Carry Trade of Japanese Yen (1980s-1990s)

One of the most well-known instances of a profitable carry trading method is the yen carry trade. Japan's central bank maintained interest rates close to zero throughout the 1980s and 1990s in an effort to fend off deflation and promote economic expansion. Because investors could borrow yen at cheap interest rates and use the money to invest in higher-yielding assets elsewhere, this provided a perfect climate for carry trades. The tactic gained so much traction that it had a big impact on international financial markets. For example, throughout the 1990s, the US stock market was supported in part by the capital inflow into US assets. But there were hazards associated with the plan. Many investors in the carry trade suffered large losses as a result of the 1997–1998 Asian financial crisis and the yen's subsequent rise in value.

2. The 2007–2008 Global Financial Crisis

Carry trades underwent a significant sea change during the global financial crisis. Low interest rates in Japan and other industrialized nations had encouraged a significant build-up of carry trades prior to the crisis. Investors made investments in high-yielding assets in emerging nations while taking out loans in low-interest currencies like the Swiss franc and yen. But these trades saw a dramatic reversal as a result of the crisis. Investors scrambled to unwind their holdings as the world's financial markets crashed, paying back their low-interest loans and liquidating high-yielding assets. As a result, emerging market assets saw a precipitous collapse while financing currencies like the yen and Swiss franc appreciated quickly. The financial crisis was made more severe by the unwinding of carry transactions, which increased volatility.

3. The 2010–2012 European Sovereign Debt Crisis

Another pivotal moment for carry trading was the issue around European national debt. Low-interest euro loans and higher-yielding government bonds from peripheral Eurozone nations like Greece, Spain, and Italy had been purchased by investors. The carry trades collapsed when these countries were confronted with dire budgetary difficulties and default danger. Bond yields for the impacted countries spiked and the euro fell sharply as investors swiftly withdrew from their positions. This time frame brought to light the dangers of carry trading, especially the exposure to sovereign credit risk.

4. The Shock of the Swiss Franc (2015)

The decision made by the Swiss National Bank (SNB) to abandon its currency peg to the euro in January 2015 was another momentous occasion in the history of carry trade. Investors had been making loans in Swiss francs for years, taking advantage of the SNB's strategy of keeping the value of the franc pegged at par with the euro. Those who were involved in carry trades involving the Swiss franc suffered significant losses as a result of the abrupt lifting of this cap, which caused the currency to appreciate dramatically. This incident served as a reminder of how crucial central bank policies are in determining the dynamics of carry trades and how quickly and unexpectedly changes could affect the strategy.

5. From 2020 onwards, the COVID-19 Pandemic

The COVID-19 pandemic has affected carry trades significantly. The global central banks' extraordinary monetary easing, which included practically zero interest rates and massive asset purchases, made carry trades more attractive. In an effort to profit from the economic recovery, investors borrowed money in low-interest currencies and made investments in assets with higher yields. But the pandemic also brought about a great deal of uncertainty and volatility, as well as abrupt changes in market sentiment. The environment surrounding carry trading is still changing as central banks modify their policies in reaction to the economic effects of the pandemic.

Chapter 3. Mechanics of Carry Trade

- Understanding Interest Rate
Differentials
- The Role of Currency Volatility
- How Carry Trades are Executed

Understanding Interest Rate Differentials

Interest rate differentials are the foundation of carry trade strategies. In essence, a carry trade involves borrowing money in a currency with a low-interest rate and investing it in a currency with a higher interest rate. The profit, or carry, comes from the difference between the lower borrowing cost and the higher investment return.

To understand this concept, let's break it down:

1. Borrowing in a Low-Interest Currency: Investors begin by borrowing funds in a currency where the central bank has set low-interest rates. For instance, the Japanese yen (JPY) and the Swiss franc (CHF) have historically had low-interest rates due to their central banks' policies aimed at stimulating economic growth and combating deflation. These low rates make it cheap to borrow in these currencies.

2. Investing in a High-Interest Currency: The borrowed funds are then converted into a currency where interest rates are higher. Emerging markets or countries with higher inflation rates often offer higher interest rates to attract investment. Examples include the Australian dollar (AUD) or the Brazilian real (BRL), where the central banks might have higher rates to control inflation or attract foreign capital.

3. Earning the Interest Differential: The core of the carry trade strategy is to earn the interest rate differential. If the borrowing rate in Japan is 0.5% and the investment rate in Brazil is 6%, the interest differential is 5.5%. This differential represents the potential profit from the carry trade, assuming currency exchange rates remain stable.

4. Leverage: To amplify returns, traders often use leverage, meaning they borrow more money than they actually have. Leverage increases both potential profits and risks. For example, using a leverage ratio of 10:1 means that for every $1 of their own money, traders borrow $10. If the trade goes as planned, the returns are significantly higher. However, if the trade goes against them, losses are also magnified.

Interest rate differentials are not static; they fluctuate based on central bank policies, economic conditions, and geopolitical events. Traders must continually monitor these factors to manage risks and identify profitable opportunities.

The Role of Currency Volatility

Currency volatility plays a crucial role in the success or failure of carry trades. While interest rate differentials provide the potential for profit, currency movements can significantly impact the returns. Here's how currency volatility factors into carry trades:

1. Exchange Rate Risk: When engaging in a carry trade, the investor is exposed to exchange rate risk. If the currency in which the investor borrowed appreciates significantly against the currency in which they invested, the gains from the interest rate differential can be wiped out or even turn into losses. For instance, if an investor

borrows in yen and invests in Australian dollars, a sudden appreciation of the yen against the Australian dollar can lead to substantial losses when converting the investment back into yen.

2. Stable Environments: Carry trades are most attractive in environments where exchange rates are relatively stable. Low volatility means that exchange rates do not fluctuate significantly, reducing the risk of adverse currency movements. Central bank policies, geopolitical stability, and predictable economic conditions contribute to such environments. Traders seek periods of low volatility to ensure that the interest rate differential is not eroded by currency fluctuations.

3. High Volatility Risks: In contrast, high volatility poses significant risks to carry trades. Sudden and sharp movements in exchange rates can lead to rapid unwinding of carry trades as investors rush to cover

their positions, leading to further market instability. Events such as financial crises, unexpected central bank interventions, or geopolitical conflicts can trigger such volatility. For example, during the 2008 financial crisis, the yen appreciated sharply as investors unwound carry trades, seeking safety in the yen.

4. Risk Management: Successful carry traders employ various risk management techniques to mitigate the impact of currency volatility. These include stop-loss orders, options, and other hedging strategies to limit potential losses. Diversification across multiple currencies and assets can also reduce the impact of volatility on the overall portfolio.

5. Carry Trade Unwind: A significant risk in carry trades is the potential for a rapid unwind. When volatility spikes, investors may rush to exit their positions to avoid further losses. This creates a feedback loop,

where selling pressure leads to further currency appreciation, exacerbating losses. Understanding market sentiment and being able to anticipate or quickly react to such scenarios is critical for carry traders.

How Carry Trades are Executed

Executing a carry trade involves several steps, from identifying the right currencies to managing the position throughout its lifecycle. Here's a detailed look at how carry trades are executed:

1. Research and Analysis: The first step is thorough research and analysis. Traders analyze global interest rates, economic indicators, and geopolitical conditions to identify potential currencies for carry trades. They look for currencies with a significant interest rate differential and stable economic conditions. Tools such as economic calendars, central bank reports,

and financial news play a crucial role in this analysis.

2. Selecting Currency Pairs: Based on the analysis, traders select the currency pair for the carry trade. For example, a trader might decide to borrow Japanese yen and invest in Australian dollars. The choice of currency pairs depends on the interest rate differential, historical volatility, and current market conditions.

3. Borrowing Funds: The next step is borrowing funds in the low-interest currency. This can be done through various financial instruments such as margin accounts, short-term loans, or derivatives. For institutional investors, borrowing can involve more complex arrangements such as currency swaps.

4. Converting and Investing: Once the funds are borrowed, they are converted into the high-interest currency. This conversion is

typically done through the foreign exchange (forex) market, where traders buy the target currency using the borrowed currency. The converted funds are then invested in high-yielding assets such as government bonds

Chapter 4. Economic Impact

- Influence on Global Financial Markets
- Effects on National Economies
- Case Studies of Economic Impact

Influence on Global Financial Markets

Carry trades have a significant impact on international financial markets, influencing how bonds, currencies, and other asset classes behave. They have a wide-ranging effect that has the potential to drastically alter market dynamics. Here is a detailed examination of the impact of carry trades on international financial markets:

1. Currency values: Carry transactions have an immediate effect on values of currencies. A high-interest currency appreciates in value when investors borrow money in a low-interest currency and invest it in a

high-interest currency. On the other hand, if supply grows, the low-interest currency can lose value. For instance, the Japanese yen frequently weakens vs other currencies as a result of heavy carry trading. Significant currency rate swings brought on by this phenomena may have an impact on global investment and trade flows.

2. Liquidity and Volatility: Carry trades can increase market liquidity, especially in the currencies and assets they target. This is because they bring in a large amount of capital. Increased liquidity helps stabilize prices and lower transaction costs in general. Carry trades, however, can potentially heighten volatility, particularly in situations where sizable positions unwind quickly. Carry trade reversals that occur suddenly can cause abrupt changes in asset prices and currency rates, as was the case in the 2008 financial crisis.

3. Interest Rate Policies: Carry traders keep a careful eye on central banks' interest rate policies. Carry trade activity can be very active in response to real or anticipated changes in interest rates, which can have considerable impact on international financial markets. In the event that the Bank of Japan keeps interest rates low and the Federal Reserve suggests a raise, for example, this could lead to carry trades that favor the US dollar over the yen. These kinds of actions have the potential to affect central banks' future policy choices when they take carry trade flows' wider economic effects into account.

4. Asset Prices and Investment Flows: Investment flows into high-yielding assets including real estate, emerging market bonds, and stocks can be influenced by carry trades. The receiving countries' economies may be stimulated and asset prices raised by these inflows. If the inflows are large and unsupported by underlying economic

factors, they may potentially result in asset bubbles. The abrupt removal of carry trade capital has the potential to cause significant asset price corrections, which would be detrimental to investor confidence and the stability of the economy.

5. Speculative Trading and Hedge Funds: A substantial portion of carry trades are executed by speculative traders and hedge funds. Their actions have the potential to intensify market fluctuations and fuel panic or frenzy episodes. These traders frequently employ leverage and complex algorithms, which can cause abrupt and significant changes in market positions. The impact of hedge funds on carry trades highlights the potential for systemic hazards and the interdependence of the world's financial markets.

Effects on National Economies

Carry trades have an economic impact on national economies in a variety of ways that go beyond financial markets. Depending on the size of carry trade activity and the surrounding economic environment, the consequences may be either good or negative. An examination of how carry trades impact national economies is provided below:

1. money Inflows and Outflows: Carry trades have the potential to bring in large amounts of money into nations with high interest rates. These inflows have the potential to stimulate economic development, provide liquidity, and encourage domestic investment. For instance, carry trades frequently lead to a rise in foreign investment in emerging markets with favorable interest rates. But these inflows can also lead to vulnerabilities and dependency because abrupt withdrawals can cause financial crises and destabilize the economy.

2. Exchange Rate Stability: The stability of a nation's exchange rate can be impacted by extensive carry trade operations. The sustained strengthening of the national currency as a result of carry trade inflows can have a negative impact on export competitiveness, trade balances, and economic growth. On the other hand, fast depreciation during carry trade unwinds may result in higher import prices and inflationary pressures. Monetary policy may become more complex if central banks are required to intervene in the currency markets in order to control these swings.

3. Interest Rate Policy: A nation's interest rate policy may be impacted by carry trade activity. The effects of interest rate decisions made by central banks on carry trade operations and the related capital flows may be taken into account. A central bank might, for example, postpone raising interest rates in order to prevent drawing in excess carry

trade inflows that might overheat the economy or cause asset bubbles. On the other hand, as carry trades unwind, they may increase rates to stop capital flight.

4. Financial industry Stability : Carry trade activity can have a big impact on the financial industry. Carry traders, such as banks and other financial institutions, can make more money when the market is favorable, but they also run a big risk when it is not. Financial institutions' balance sheets may be strained by significant losses from carry trades, which could result in more widespread financial instability. In order to control the risks involved in carry trades and guarantee the stability of the financial industry, regulatory actions might be required.

5. Economic Cycles: By magnifying capital flows and investment patterns, carry trades have the potential to worsen economic cycles. Carry trades can encourage excessive

loan growth and asset price inflation during times of low volatility and economic boom. On the other hand, the unwinding of carry trades might cause abrupt contractions in asset prices and credit availability during times of high volatility or economic downturn, which would exacerbate the situation.

Case Studies of Economic Impact

Let's look at a few noteworthy case studies that demonstrate the various consequences of carry trades on national economies and financial markets in order to demonstrate their economic impact:

1. The Carry Trade of Yen with Japan: Carry trades in yen have been one of the most well-known types of trading. For many years, investors were encouraged to borrow in yen and put their money into higher-yielding assets overseas by Japan's

low interest rate environment. This resulted in large capital outflows and a continuous weakening of the yen. Although the carry trade made cash inexpensive for international investments, it left Japan vulnerable. The quick unwinding of yen carry trades during times of financial strain, like the 2008 financial crisis, caused the yen to appreciate sharply, escalating deflationary pressures and impeding Japan's economic recovery.

2. The 2008 Icelandic Financial Crisis: Carry trades contributed to a notable influx of foreign cash into Iceland throughout the early 2000s. Attracted by Iceland's high interest rates, investors borrowed money in low-interest currencies like the Swiss franc and yen to invest in Icelandic assets. The economic boom that resulted from this capital inflow was marked by a sharp increase in credit and asset prices. But the carry trade money swiftly reversed when the global financial crisis struck in 2008,

causing a serious financial disaster in Iceland. The banking industry failed, the Icelandic krona fell precipitously, and a severe recession gripped the country.

3. Brazil and the Real: Because of its historically high interest rates, Brazil has frequently been the focus of carry trades. Carry trade inflows strengthened the real, the Brazilian currency, and promoted economic expansion during times of international economic stability. These inflows did, however, bring with them certain difficulties, such as how export competitiveness was impacted by currency appreciation and how inflation was increased. Carry trade outflows caused a significant devaluation of the real when international conditions shifted, as they did during the 2013 "Taper Tantrum" when the U.S. Federal Reserve signaled a slowdown in its asset purchases. This increased inflationary pressures and economic instability.

4. Turkey and the Lira: Carry trades have also had an impact on Turkey. High interest rates drew in international investment, which strengthened the Turkish currency and promoted economic expansion. But Turkey was susceptible to carry trade reversals because of its substantial external debt, coupled with political and economic concerns. The lira has sharply depreciated in recent years due to bouts of carry trade unwinding, which has raised inflation and posed serious hurdles for the Turkish economy.

Chapter 5. Real-Life Examples

- The Yen Carry Trade
- The Icelandic Financial Crisis
- The Role of Emerging Markets

The Yen Carry Trade

One of the most well-known applications of a carry trade strategy is the yen carry trade, which takes advantage of Japan's historically low interest rates to make investments in higher-yielding assets globally. The Japanese yen's stability and predictability, along with Japan's long-standing low or negative interest rate policies, have made this trade quite popular.

1. Mechanics of the Yen Carry Trade: By utilizing Japan's cheap borrowing costs, investors borrow money in Japanese yen. After that, they exchange these funds for a currency that has a higher interest rate—like

the Australian dollar—and use that currency to buy assets. The differential between the cheap borrowing costs in yen and the higher returns on invested assets is what generates the profits.

2. Impact on Financial Markets: The carry trade in yen has the potential to cause large capital inflows into assets and currencies with higher yields. This pushes down on the yen while simultaneously increasing demand for those currencies and causing them to appreciate. For instance, significant carry trade flows in the mid-2000s caused the yen to drop and the Australian dollar and the euro to appreciate.

3. Dangers and Turnarounds: Currency volatility is the main risk associated with the yen carry trade. Investors holding debt denominated in yen may incur higher repayment costs if the yen appreciates significantly. This risk became apparent in

the midst of the 2008 global financial crisis, when investors unwound their carry trade positions, taking refuge in the yen's perceived stability. This led to a large appreciation of the yen. This abrupt turn of events resulted in significant losses for numerous carry traders and added to the instability of the world market.

4. Long-Term Implications: Japan and the international financial system have both long-term effects from the yen carry trade. The ongoing yen devaluation has impacted Japan's ability to compete internationally and its ability to make economic policy decisions. The carry trade has demonstrated the interdependence of financial markets worldwide and the possibility of systemic dangers in the event that large-scale trades abruptly terminate.

The Icelandic Financial Crisis

Carry trades can lead to economic booms and crashes, as the 2008 Icelandic financial crisis amply illustrates. In the early 2000s, carry trade investments gained popularity in Iceland due to its liberal financial rules and high interest rates.

1. Pre-Crisis Economic Boom: Significant foreign capital inflows drove Iceland's economy to grow rapidly in the years preceding the crisis. Drawn by Iceland's high interest rates, investors borrowed money in low-interest currencies like the Swiss franc and Japanese yen and invested in Icelandic assets. A thriving economy, increasing asset prices, and rapid credit expansion were the results of this capital inflow.

2. Bubble Formation: The stock market and real estate bubbles were fueled in part by money inflows. Thanks to the plethora of foreign money available, Icelandic banks made rapid local and worldwide expansions.

The assets of the banking industry increased to multiple times the GDP of the nation, resulting in a highly leveraged and precarious financial system.

3. Crisis Unfolding: A significant turnaround was brought about by the 2008 global financial crisis. As investors became more risk averse and global liquidity dried up, they started unwinding their carry trade bets. As a result, asset values plummeted and the Icelandic krona saw a severe depreciation. Due to its heavy reliance on short-term foreign investment, Iceland's banking industry had a serious liquidity problem before collapsing.

4. Economic Fallout: There were serious economic repercussions from the Icelandic financial crisis. A severe recession, skyrocketing unemployment, and severe economic misery for the populace resulted from the banking sector's collapse. For the economy to stabilize, the government was

forced to impose austerity measures and apply for emergency assistance from the International Monetary Fund (IMF). The crisis brought to light the dangers of carry trades and the significance of prudent risk management and financial regulation.

The Role of Emerging Markets

Carry trades have frequently targeted emerging markets because of their higher interest rates and prospects for growth. These transactions include a risk of volatility and capital flight, but they can also result in significant capital inflows and accelerate economic growth.

1. Attractiveness of Emerging Markets: Carry trade investments are drawn to emerging markets because they usually provide greater interest rates than industrialized ones. Investors seeking larger profits have frequently picked nations like

South Africa, Brazil, and Turkey. These influxes have the potential to stabilize local currencies, fund infrastructure improvements, and promote economic growth.

2. Economic Advantages and Hazards: Carry trade capital inflows have the potential to boost investment, asset prices, and emerging market economic indices. They do, however, also have hazards. Financial instability, capital flight, and severe currency depreciations can result from abrupt reversals of carry trading positions. For instance, carry trade activities have caused notable volatility in the real and lira of Brazil and Turkey, respectively.

3. Research Case: Brazil: Brazil's high interest rates have made it a popular location for carry trades. Carry trade inflows have benefited the economy by sustaining the Brazilian real's appreciation during times of economic stability. Yet, external

shocks have caused sharp outflows and currency devaluation, such as adjustments in US monetary policy. Significant outflows from Brazil occurred during the 2013 "Taper Tantrum," when the U.S. Federal Reserve hinted at tapering its quantitative easing program. This sharply depreciated the real and economic issues.

4. Regulatory Reactions: To control the risks involved with carry trades, emerging market nations have created a number of regulatory initiatives. These consist include monetary policy changes, capital controls, and involvement in the foreign exchange markets. Brazil, for example, has imposed taxes on short-term foreign investments in an effort to lessen the volatility brought on by carry trades.

5. Long-Term Considerations: Carry trades draw attention to the significance of sound financial regulation and sustainable economic policies, even though they can

have short-term positive economic effects. Managing the risks of abrupt capital withdrawals must be balanced with luring in foreign investment for emerging markets. Resilient financial systems, diverse funding sources, and sound macroeconomic policies are essential for reducing the negative consequences of carry trade volatility.

Chapter 6. Risk and Reward

- Potential Gains from Carry Trades
- Risks Involved in Carry Trades
- Managing and Mitigating Risks

Potential Gains from Carry Trades

Carry trades are a popular strategy among investors because they can yield significant gains. The primary allure is found in the variations in interest rates among nations, which enable investors to generate profits surpassing the expense of borrowing.

1. Interest Rate Differentials: The variance in interest rates between two currencies is the main source of profit from carry trading. An investor can profit from the difference in interest rates if, for instance, they borrow money in a low-interest currency, such as the Japanese yen, and invest it in a high-interest currency, such as the Australian dollar. This difference in interest

rates can be significant, especially when taken on leverage.

2. Leverage: In carry trades, investors frequently employ leverage to increase their gains. They can expose themselves to the interest rate differential to a greater extent by borrowing more than their original capital. Leveraging a deal, for example, by borrowing ten times the starting cash can increase prospective gains by a factor of ten. This amplifies the risks as well as the potential returns.

3. Currency Appreciation: Investors can benefit from currency appreciation in addition to the interest rate differential. The investor benefits from changes in the exchange rate if the currency they invested increases in value relative to the currency they borrowed. Carry trades are quite appealing since they offer the twin benefits

of generating interest rate spreads and possibly even making currency gains.

4. Diversification: Carry trades can be included in a portfolio that is diversified. Investors can improve their total returns by devoting a portion of their portfolio to carry trades rather than depending exclusively on conventional asset types like equities and bonds. If the carry trades are done carefully, this diversity can aid in managing the total risk of the portfolio.

5. Market Conditions: Carry trade profitability can be increased by favorable market conditions, such as low volatility and stable economic settings. The likelihood of abrupt currency swings lowers during times of low market volatility, which helps investors forecast returns and manage their positions.

Risks Involved in Carry Trades

Carry trades are risky and can result in large losses even if they might be profitable, particularly in volatile markets. It is imperative that any investor thinking about using this technique understands these dangers.

1. Currency Risk: Currency volatility is the main risk associated with carry trading. The cost of loan repayment rises if the borrowed currency gains a substantial value relative to the invested currency, potentially eliminating any advantages from interest rate differentials. For instance, an investor may suffer significant losses if they borrow money in yen and invest it in Australian dollars.

2. Interest Rate Risk: Carry transactions may be impacted by changes in interest rates. The cost of borrowing goes up and the

profit margin shrinks if the interest rate of the currency being borrowed is raised by the central bank of that currency. On the other hand, returns fall if the invested currency's central bank reduces interest rates. The state of the economy has an impact on central banks' monetary policy, and unanticipated shifts may have a negative impact on carry trades.

3. Leverage Risk: Leverage can increase profits, but it can also increase losses. Even slight negative changes in interest rates or exchange rates can result in substantial losses in highly leveraged carry bets. Leveraged positions may become unmanageable during times of strong market volatility, which could result in forced liquidation and significant financial loss.

4. Market Liquidity Risk: Carry trades are susceptible to liquidity risk, which makes it challenging to swiftly take positions or sell

them without impacting the market price. Liquidity can dry up during financial crises or times of intense market stress, making it difficult to exit investments at advantageous prices. This may make losses worse, particularly if investors are compelled to sell their holdings in a market with little liquidity.

5. Economic and Political Risk: Interest rates and currency prices may be impacted by political and economic unrest in the nations engaged in the carry trade. Unpredictable and abrupt shifts in the market might result from political events like elections, changes in policy, or tensions in the geopolitical arena. The profitability of carry trades can also be impacted by economic downturns or crises.

Managing and Mitigating Risks

Success in carry trading depends on controlling and reducing the inherent risks involved. In order to safeguard their investments and guarantee long-term profits, investors need to utilize a range of tactics and instruments.

1. Hedging Strategies: Hedging is the process of offsetting any losses in carry trades with financial instruments. Investors can protect themselves against unfavorable currency fluctuations, for instance, by using options, futures, or forward contracts. Investors can preserve their upside potential while lowering their downside risk by buying options or locking in exchange rates.

2. Diversification: You can lower overall risk by spreading carry trade holdings over a variety of currencies and interest rate differentials. Investing in multiple currency pairs allows investors to diversify their holdings and lessen the impact of unfavorable fluctuations in any one pair.

This strategy can assist in distributing the portfolio's risks and benefits evenly.

3. Monitoring and Adjustment: To effectively manage carry trade risks, constant observation of the state of the market, economic data, and central bank policies is required. Investors need to be ready to modify their positions in response to shifting market conditions. This could entail lowering leverage, rebalancing the portfolio, or liquidating investments in reaction to unfavorable events.

4. Risk Management Tools: Investors can track their positions, assess their exposure to risk, and put risk control measures in place by using risk management tools and software. Sophisticated analytics and algorithms have the ability to reveal such hazards and recommend suitable measures to alleviate them.

5. Setting Stop-Loss Orders: By automatically closing positions when they hit a predefined level, stop-loss orders can assist reduce losses. This eliminates the possibility of uncontrollably large losses in deals using high leverage. As a safety net, stop-loss orders make sure that losses are kept within reasonable bounds.

6. Stress Testing and Scenario Analysis: Investors can gain insight into the performance of their carry trade positions by performing scenario analysis and stress tests. Simulating a range of situations, including extreme ones, allows investors to evaluate possible risks and create backup strategies. Being proactive improves resilience and readiness.

7. Responsible Use of Leverage: Although leverage can increase returns, it must be utilized carefully. Before using leverage, investors should carefully consider their financial capabilities and risk tolerance.

Keeping enough margin and employing modest amounts of leverage can assist control the dangers involved with more leveraged positions.

8. Regulatory Awareness: Managing carry trade risks necessitates keeping up with regulatory changes and compliance requirements. Restrictions or limitations that affect carry trade activity may be imposed by regulatory bodies. Complying with these restrictions and modifying tactics appropriately can help avoid financial and legal issues.

Chapter 7. Carry Trade in Practice

- Institutional vs. Retail Investors
- Strategies Employed by Hedge Funds
- Tools and Platforms for Executing Carry Trades

Institutional vs. Retail Investors

Both institutional and retail investors use carry trades as a common strategy, although their methods and resources are very different.

Financial Advisors

Institutional investors possess substantial resources at their disposal, including mutual funds, hedge funds, and pension funds. Large capital bases, complex trading systems, and access to a variety of financial markets and products are among their advantages.

1. Capital and Leverage: Institutional investors can increase profits by utilizing their substantial capital bases. They can negotiate advantageous borrowing conditions and have access to large credit lines. They are able to increase the interest rate differentials they obtain from carry trades as a result.

2. Advanced Technology and Systems: To find and execute carry trades effectively, these investors make use of cutting-edge trading platforms and algorithms. They may take advantage of minute market swings and execute deals quickly thanks to high-frequency trading technologies.

3. Research and Analysis: Specialized research teams employed by institutional investors examine movements in interest rates, economic data, and geopolitical

developments. They are better able to anticipate market fluctuations that may affect their carry trade holdings and make well-informed judgments thanks to this thorough analysis.

4. Risk Management: Institutional investors require strong risk management frameworks. They evaluate and reduce the risks connected to carry trades using complex models. These models take into account variables including interest rate fluctuations, currency volatility, and liquidity situations.

Investors in Retail

Conversely, retail investors usually have less access to sophisticated trading instruments and fewer resources available to them. They can still take part in carry trades, though, in a number of ways.

1. Access to Information: Broker research reports, publicly available data, and financial news are the main sources of information for retail investors. They might make use of internet trading systems that give them access to analytical tools and real-time data.

2. Leverage: Although retail investors are able to employ leverage, their credit options are frequently more constrained than those of institutional investors. The amount of leverage they are able to utilize may be limited by the margin restrictions that brokers establish.

3. Simpler techniques: Purchasing higher-yielding currencies and holding them for interest rate gains are examples of simpler carry trade techniques that are frequently used by retail investors. They might not use a lot of derivatives or complicated hedging strategies.

4. Risk Management: When it comes to risk management, retail investors need to use caution. They can diversify their currency holdings to lower risk exposure and establish stop-loss orders to limit any losses. They might not have as advanced of risk management techniques as institutional investors, though.

Strategies Employed by Hedge Funds

Hedge funds are renowned for using complex and aggressive trading techniques. In the world of carry trades, they use a variety of strategies to control risk and optimize returns.

1. Leveraged Carry Trades: To increase the gains from interest rate differentials, hedge funds frequently employ large leverage. They can increase their gains by taking out loans that are substantially larger than their

original capital. But this also makes them more vulnerable to risk.

2. Currency Pairs: Interest rate differentials, economic fundamentals, and geopolitical considerations are taken into careful consideration by hedge funds when choosing currency pairs. They frequently aim for currencies with steady economies and dependable monetary policy.

3. Dynamic Positioning: Hedge funds modify their exposure in response to market conditions as they actively manage their carry trade holdings. In reaction to shifts in interest rates, the release of economic data, or developments in geopolitics, they can take a stronger or lower stance.

4. Hedging Techniques: Hedge funds employ a variety of hedging strategies to reduce risks. They include futures and options agreements to hedge against unfavorable fluctuations in exchange rates.

They might also insure against interest rate risk by using cross-currency swaps.

5. Algorithmic Trading: To execute carry bets, a lot of hedge firms employ algorithmic trading techniques. These algorithms take advantage of market inefficiencies and reduce the influence of human emotions on trading decisions by analyzing enormous volumes of data and executing transactions quickly.

6. Global Macro Strategies: Global macro strategies, which take into account broader economic patterns and geopolitical developments, are frequently utilized by hedge funds. They adopt stances in response to projected shifts in interest rates, global economic expansion, and political stability.

Tools and Platforms for Executing Carry Trades

Carry trade execution is made easier by a number of instruments and platforms available to both institutional and retail participants. The real-time data, analytical power, and execution methods that these technologies offer are essential for profitable trading.

1. Online Trading Platforms: Retail investors can access currency markets using platforms such as Interactive Brokers, MetaTrader, and Thinkorswim. These platforms offer order execution capabilities, charting tools, and real-time quotes.

2. Algorithmic Trading Systems: Sophisticated algorithmic trading systems that automate carry transaction execution are frequently used by institutional investors. These systems find trading opportunities, evaluate market data, and quickly execute deals.

3. Research and Analysis platforms: For both institutional and individual investors, platforms like Bloomberg Terminal and Reuters Eikon offer extensive data and analytical capabilities. To assist traders in making wise judgments, these systems provide news feeds, economic statistics, and interest rate projections.

4. Risk Management tools: Investors can evaluate and control the risks involved with carry trades with the use of risk management tools, such as Bloomberg's PORT and MSCI's RiskMetrics. These resources offer perceptions into interest rate risk, currency volatility, and liquidity situations.

5. Hedging Instruments: Carry trade positions can be hedged using a variety of financial instruments, including swaps, futures, and options. These products offer flexibility in risk management because they

can be traded on exchanges or over-the-counter markets.

6. Mobile Trading Apps: Carry trades can be easily executed on the fly with the use of mobile trading apps for ordinary investors. Applications such as ETRADE, Robinhood, and TD Ameritrade Mobile give users access to real-time data, order execution, and currency markets.

7. Economic Calendars: These offer details about forthcoming economic gatherings, including interest rate decisions, central bank meetings, and the release of economic statistics. These calendars aid traders in predicting changes in the market and modifying their positions accordingly.

8. Backtesting Tools: By utilizing historical data, backtesting tools let investors test their carry trade ideas. This aids in evaluating the strategy's possible dangers and profitability before to putting it into

practice in real markets. TradingView and QuantConnect are two platforms that allow for backtesting.

Chapter 8. Myths and Misconceptions

- Common Misunderstandings about Carry Trades
- Debunking Popular Myths
- Realities vs. Perceptions

Common Misunderstandings about Carry Trades

In the world of finance, carry trades are a complicated and sometimes misinterpreted tactic. Carry trades are popular among institutional and retail investors alike, but there are still a number of widespread misconceptions regarding their operation and its benefits and hazards. Anyone thinking about using this investment strategy has to be aware of these misconceptions.

1. Carry Trades Offer No Risk: The idea that carry trades are a risk-free method of making money is among the most widespread misconceptions. The reason for this misperception is probably that the plan looks simple: borrow money in a currency with a low interest rate and invest it in a currency with a high interest rate. This, however, ignores the important risks that could result in substantial losses, such as interest rate fluctuations and currency volatility.

2. Carry Trades Always Yield Positive profits: Another misconception is that the interest rate differential ensures that carry trades will always result in positive profits. Exchange rate changes have the ability to reduce or even eliminate potential profits, even though the interest rate differential is the foundation for them. The exchange may result in a net loss if the financing currency

depreciates sufficiently in relation to the high-yielding currency.

3. Carry Trades are Only for vast Institutions: Retail investors can engage in carry trades, but institutional investors are the most well-known participants since they have access to vast capital bases and sophisticated trading instruments. Retail investors can participate in carry trades using a variety of online trading platforms, but with varying risk management and capital limits.

4. Carry Trades Cause Market Instability: According to some, carry trades cause financial markets to become intrinsically unstable. Although carry trade unwinding on a big scale might exacerbate volatility, market instability is not exclusively the result of this technique. Numerous factors, such as economic data, geopolitical developments, and central bank policy, can affect market movements.

5. Carry Trades: An Effective Short-Term Approach It's a common misperception that carry trades are only appropriate for quick transactions. Carry trades can, in fact, be used as long-term or short-term trading techniques. If the economic fundamentals backing the trade continue to be good, investors may keep positions for extended periods of time in order to profit from continuous interest rate differentials.

Debunking Popular Myths

It's critical to dispel these misconceptions and comprehend the actual workings of the technique in order to make wise selections regarding carry trades.

1. The Fallacy of Profits Without Risk: Carry trades do not come without risk. The main hazards include changes in interest rates, currency volatility, and geopolitical events.

Investors need to understand that abrupt changes in economic conditions or market mood can cause exchange rates to fluctuate quickly, with the potential for large losses. To reduce these risks, it is essential to practice effective risk management, which includes hedging strategies and the use of stop-loss orders.

2. currency Rate Impact: The idea that carry trades are always profitable overlooks the influence of fluctuations in currency rates. For instance, if an investor borrows money in Australian dollars (high interest) and invests it in Japanese yen (low interest), a sudden decline in the value of the Australian dollar relative to the yen could cancel out the interest rate gains and result in a loss. As a result, keeping an eye on economic data and exchange rate fluctuations is essential for profitable carry trading.

3. Accessibility for ordinary Investors: Although carry trades are mostly made by

large institutions, ordinary investors are welcome to take part. Leveraged trading accounts are provided by many brokers, enabling regular investors to borrow money and execute carry trades. Retail investors should use caution, though, as excessive leverage increases the possibility of both losses and gains. For retail investors, conducting thorough research, comprehending market dynamics, and exercising cautious risk management are crucial.

4. Carry Trades and Market Instability: It is oversimplified to say that carry trades lead to market instability. Carry trade unwinding can cause volatility, however this is typically the outcome of more general market dynamics. For example, unwinding carry transactions during the 2008 global financial crisis was not the primary cause of market instability; rather, it was an aggravating factor. Market instability frequently results from a variety of causes,

such as shifts in policy, credit crises, and economic recessions.

5. Temporal versus Long-Term Approach: Carry trades are flexible enough to accommodate both short- and long-term time frames. While long-term investors may maintain positions for longer periods of time to benefit from continuous interest rate advantages, short-term traders may profit from transient interest rate differentials and swift market changes. The strategy must be in line with the investor's investing objectives, market forecast, and risk tolerance.

Realities vs. Perceptions

Recognizing myths from reality is crucial for successful carry trade navigation. Investors may make wise selections and efficiently manage their investments by being aware of the strategy's genuine nature.

1. Reality of Risk: It is false to believe that carry trades are low-risk. contain trades do, in fact, contain a number of risks, such as interest rate risk, currency risk, and geopolitical risk. Investors need to be ready for possible losses, use risk management techniques, and perform extensive research. Some of these risks can be reduced by employing hedging tools and diversifying currency positions.

2. real Returns: Although there is a chance for positive returns due to the interest rate differential, real results are contingent on a number of variables. Changes in exchange rates have a significant impact on how profitable carry trades are. Investors should keep an eye on global events, central bank policy, and economic data as these can all affect currency values. Unrealistic expectations might arise when interest rate differentials are the only factor taken into account, neglecting other market variables.

3. Accessibility and Tools: It's no longer true that carry trades are exclusive to big organizations. Technology developments and internet trading platforms have made currency markets more accessible to a wider audience. Carry trades are now open to retail investors, but they need to utilize the right tools and approach the technique cautiously. Retail investors can benefit from broker-provided risk management features, trading platforms, and educational materials to assist them understand the intricacies of carry trades.

4. Impact on Markets: Carry trades have a complex effect on market stability. Carry trade unwinding is typically a symptom of market instability rather than the cause, though it can occasionally add to short-term volatility. Market fluctuations are frequently influenced by policy changes, financial crises, and broader economic situations. Carry trades should be considered by

investors in the larger context of market dynamics, and they should be ready for possible volatility.

5. Strategic Flexibility: Carry trades allow for a flexible investment horizon. Based on their view for the market and risk tolerance, investors can choose between short-term and long-term plans. While long-term investors may keep positions to profit from long-term interest rate advantages, short-term traders may look to profit quickly on transient interest rate differentials. Success hinges on tailoring the plan to each person's tastes and the state of the market.

Chapter 9. Popular Beliefs and Cultural Impact

- The Carry Trade in Financial Media
- Cultural Perceptions and Misperceptions
- Carry Trades in Pop Culture

The Carry Trade in Financial Media

The carry trade has received a lot of attention in the financial media because of its unique combination of global economics and big profit possibilities. Carry trades are a common topic of discussion among financial journalists, analysts, and pundits, who emphasize both their benefits and drawbacks. The way that this intricate financial strategy is perceived and understood by the general public is greatly influenced by media coverage.

1. Media Emphasis on Profitability: By presenting successful case studies and

stressing the possibility of large returns, financial media frequently highlights the profitability of carry trades. Stories of investors who have profited greatly from taking advantage of currency interest rate differentials are common in articles and publications. This emphasis on profitability may overlook the risks involved with carry trades and provide the false impression that they are a reliable way to generate significant returns.

2. Risk Analysis: Although profits are the primary focus, credible financial media also offer in-depth examinations of the hazards associated with carry trades. Analysts talk about how carry trade positions are affected by economic fluctuations, geopolitical developments, and currency volatility. Investors can better understand that although carry trades can be profitable, there are considerable dangers associated with them thanks to this fair coverage.

Financial media frequently stresses the value of risk management techniques and urges care.

3. Real-Time Updates and Alerts: Carry trade conditions are subject to sudden changes due to the dynamic nature of financial markets. Real-time information and notifications on interest rate decisions, currency fluctuations, and economic data are provided by financial media outlets. For investors making carry trades, these updates are essential because they allow them to make well-informed judgments based on the most recent movements in the market.

4. Educational Content: To assist investors in understanding carry trades, a number of financial media sites provide educational content. This contains thorough explanations of carry trade operations, the variables affecting their profitability, and helpful guidance on carrying transaction execution. Financial media can encourage a

wider audience to think about include carry trades in their investment portfolio by demythologizing the technique.

Cultural Perceptions and Misperceptions

Like many financial techniques, carry trades are prone to misconceptions and differing cultural views. Historical occurrences, regional economic situations, and the general public's degree of financial awareness can all have an impact on these opinions.

1. Views in Developed Economies: Carry trades are frequently viewed as complex investment methods used by seasoned traders and financial institutions in developed markets like the US, the UK, and Japan. Because of the high degree of financial awareness in these areas, carry trades are widely recognized as involving

high risk and needing to be managed carefully. Still, there may be a belief that carry trades are mainly the purview of wealthy investors.

2. Illogical Beliefs in Developing Markets: Carry trades may be seen as enigmatic or too complicated in emerging markets where there may be a lack of financial awareness. The dangers associated with these trades and how they operate are frequently misunderstood. Carry trades could occasionally be looked with suspicion, particularly if they are thought to be a factor in economic instability or currency volatility. It is crucial to debunk misconceptions and encourage well-informed decision-making by teaching investors in these areas about the workings and dangers of carry trades.

3. Historical Context: Carry trades might be perceived differently by cultures according to historical occurrences. For instance, the

yen carry trade gained significant popularity in Japan between the 1990s and the beginning of the 2000s. The plan was to invest in higher-yielding currencies and borrow yen at low interest rates. Even though a lot of investors made money, there were major market disruptions when these deals were later unwound at times when the yen appreciated. Because of this background, Japanese investors are now more wary of carry trades and cognizant of the risks involved.

4. Impact of Financial Crises: Carry trades have also been viewed differently in culture as a result of financial crises, such as the global financial crisis of 2008. The unwinding of carry transactions intensified financial instability and increased market volatility throughout the crisis. Both institutional and ordinary investors now approach carry trades with greater caution as a result of this. The lessons from past crises emphasize how critical it is to

comprehend carry trades' possible systemic dangers as well as the larger economic environment.

Carry Trades in Pop Culture

Carry trades are mostly a financial technique, but they have also influenced larger societal myths about investing and finance, as evidenced by their appearance in popular culture.

1. Portrayal in Films and Television Series: Wall Street and high finance-related films and television series occasionally highlight financial tactics such as carry trades. Carry trades are one of the sophisticated financial instruments and trading methods that are explored in TV shows like "Billions" and movies like "The Big Short". In addition to adding to the mystery and intrigue underlying carry trades, these depictions may emphasize or oversimplify the tactic for entertainment value. Even though these

depictions have the potential to increase awareness, they frequently fall short of giving a thorough grasp of the dangers and intricacies involved.

2. References in Literature and Journalism: Financial journalism and literature occasionally make reference to carry trades. Carry trades are frequently covered in books and articles that explore the complexities of global finance as part of larger stories on currency markets and investing techniques. By offering background information and commentary that goes beyond dramatic headlines, these references can aid in demystifying carry trades for a larger audience.

3. Influence on Investor Behavior: How carry trades are portrayed in popular culture has the potential to affect how investors behave, especially small-time investors. Carry trades can pique the curiosity of investors hoping to replicate the success of

fictitious or real-life figures when they are presented as extremely profitable and complex trading techniques. This curiosity needs to be restrained, though, by a realistic awareness of the dangers. When it comes to giving correct information and assisting in the making of well-informed decisions, financial media and educational resources are essential.

4. Celebrity Investors and Influencers: With the growth of social media, these individuals now have a platform to discuss a range of financial techniques, including carry trades. Some influencers downplay the hazards or oversimplify the strategy, while others offer insightful commentary. Investors need to look for reliable and informed specialists and thoroughly assess the information they learn from various sources.

Chapter 10. Case Studies

- Successful Carry Trade Strategies
- High-Profile Failures
- Lessons Learned from Past Trades

Successful Carry Trade Strategies

Carry trades have been a mainstay of international financial strategies for a long time, and their potential for significant gains has been demonstrated by many success stories. These profitable transactions frequently demonstrate how to use interest rate differentials, market timing, and risk management strategically.

1. The Early 2000s Yen Carry Trade:
The early 2000s yen carry trade is among the most famous instances of a profitable carry trade. Because of the Bank of Japan's liberal monetary policy, investors were able to borrow Japanese yen at historically low interest rates, which they then used to invest

in higher-yielding assets like US and Australian dollars. By taking advantage of the significant interest rate difference between Japan and other nations, this technique produced significant profits for investors. A steady global economy and the low rates of the yen made this trading especially rewarding.

2. The Swiss Franc Carry Trade: Investing in higher-yielding currencies or assets while borrowing low-interest Swiss francs is another example of a successful carry trade. Early in the new millennium, Swiss franc carry trades gained popularity as a result of the low interest rate environment upheld by the Swiss National Bank. In established economies with higher interest rates, such as developing markets, investors wanted higher returns. Up until changes in the economy affected its profitability, this method was appealing because to the Swiss

franc's steadiness and cheap borrowing costs.

3. Emerging Markets Boom of 2010:
Emerging markets grew rapidly in the 2010s, and many investors used carry trades to benefit from these economies' higher interest rates than in established markets. For instance, investing in high-yielding assets in nations like Brazil and Turkey and taking out loans in low-interest currencies like the yen offered enticing rewards. As long as emerging market nations sustained economic stability and continued to offer greater rates, the carry trading strategy proved effective.

4. Managed Funds and Institutional Successes: By utilizing advanced risk management and diversification techniques, institutional investors and hedge funds have also had noteworthy success with carry trades. To find and take advantage of interest rate differences while reducing the

risks brought on by currency volatility, these funds frequently employ sophisticated models. Their proficiency in risk management, real-time data access, and large-scale transaction management are the reasons behind their success.

High-Profile Failures

Carry trades have a lot of risk involved, even though they can be quite rewarding. The possible drawbacks of this approach have been highlighted by a number of well-publicized failures, highlighting the significance of meticulous preparation and risk management.

1. The Financial Crisis in Iceland (2008):
A well-known example of a financial catastrophe associated with carry trading is Iceland. To finance high-yield investments in Iceland, Icelandic banks aggressively borrowed in low-interest currencies like the

yen and Swiss francs in the years preceding the financial crisis. The Icelandic krona saw a sharp decline in value during the 2008 global financial crisis, and the banks experienced serious liquidity problems. The crisis that resulted in the major Icelandic financial institutions collapsing and a severe economic downturn in the country was partly caused by the carry transactions unwinding quickly.

2. The 1997–1998 Asian Financial Crisis:
Carry trades using Asian currencies contributed to the worsening of the financial crisis in Asia. Investors made high-yield investments in Asian nations while taking out loans in currencies with low interest rates. Asian currencies had a rapid decline in value as a result of speculative attacks, leaving investors with large losses. Carry trades can exacerbate economic vulnerabilities, particularly in emerging nations that are seeing large inflows and

outflows of money, as the crisis demonstrated.

3. The 2015 Swiss Franc Shock: The Swiss franc experienced a strong appreciation against the euro and other currencies in January 2015 as a result of the Swiss National Bank (SNB) abruptly lifting its cap on the currency. This abrupt rise caught many carry trades, which involved borrowing in Swiss francs and investing in other currencies or assets, off guard. Due to the ensuing currency volatility, investors who had not expected such a sharp change in exchange rates suffered large losses.

4. The Volatility of the 2020 COVID-19 Market:
Carry transactions were affected globally by the extreme market volatility caused by the COVID-19 epidemic. As global markets responded to the pandemic, investors who had borrowed money in low-interest currencies and put it toward higher-yielding

assets saw abrupt and significant drops in their asset values. In reaction to the crisis, carry trades were quickly unwound, which exacerbated market volatility and brought attention to the dangers of depending on methods that rely on steady economic conditions.

Lessons Learned from Past Trades

Investors can learn a lot from the successes and failures of carry trades, especially in relation to risk management, market dynamics, and strategic planning.

1. Importance of Risk Management: Establishing strong risk management is one of the most important lessons learned from previous carry trade experiences. Profitable carry traders use techniques like stop-loss orders, investment diversification, and liquidity management to reduce possible

losses. Inadequate risk management procedures frequently lead to high-profile failures, emphasizing the necessity of thorough planning and backup plans.

2. Impact of Economic Conditions: Carry trades are extremely susceptible to shifts in monetary policy and the state of the economy. Market conditions that are steady and have predictable interest rate differentials are conducive to successful trades. On the other hand, abrupt shifts in policy, geopolitical events, or economic shocks can cause quick and unanticipated fluctuations in currency prices. In order to foresee any effects on their carry trades, investors need keep up to date on central bank policies and worldwide economic trends.

3. Market Timing Needed: Carry trades depend heavily on timing. Finding advantageous circumstances and timing trades are two skills that successful traders

frequently possess. On the other hand, ill-timed transactions can result in large losses, particularly if the market conditions change suddenly. Learning from prior mistakes highlights how crucial it is to conduct thorough market research and time carry trades.

4. Diversification and Hedging: Two crucial tactics for controlling the risks involved in carry trades are diversification and hedging. Investors may be exposed to concentrated risks if they depend only on one carry trade. To guard against unfavorable changes in exchange rates, savvy traders frequently utilize a diverse portfolio of carry trades and hedging strategies. This strategy lessens the effects of adverse market developments and helps to strike a balance between risk and return.

5. Understanding Systemic Risks : Carry trades have the ability to increase systemic risks in financial markets, as seen by

well-publicized failures. It is important for investors to understand how their transactions may affect larger market dynamics and heighten volatility. Making wise investing choices requires an understanding of systemic risks and the possible effects of carry trades on financial stability.

Chapter 11. Regulatory Environment

- How Governments and Regulators View Carry Trades
- Major Regulatory Changes Over Time
- Impact of Regulation on Carry Trade Viability

How Governments and Regulators View Carry Trades

Carry trades have long attracted the attention of governments and financial authorities because of their potential to impact market dynamics and financial stability. Carry trades can have a big impact on exchange rates, asset prices, and general market volatility since they entail borrowing money in low-interest currencies and investing it in high-yield assets.

1. Concerns About Financial Stability: Carry trades are seen negatively by regulators mainly because of the possibility that they may worsen financial instability. If circumstances abruptly shift, the enormous leverage sometimes linked to carry trades may result in severe market corrections. Market volatility may increase if there is an abrupt change in interest rates or a currency crisis, for example, which would push traders to hastily unwind their positions. This was made clear by the quick unwinding of carry trades, which caused extreme financial instability during both the 2008 Icelandic financial crisis and the Asian Financial Crisis (1997–1998).

2. Impact on currency Rates: Carry deals have the potential to significantly influence currency rates. Traders can cause currency appreciation or depreciation based on net capital flows by borrowing money at a low interest rate and investing in assets valued

in higher-yielding currencies. Because of the inflows and outflows connected to carry trades, country economies—especially those of emerging markets—may see dramatic changes in their currencies. The possibility that these trades could affect economic fundamentals and disrupt currency markets worries regulators.

3. Systemic Risk and Leverage: Regulators are quite concerned about the use of leverage in carry trades. Leverage increases the possibility for both gains and losses. It can also cause a cascade of instability in the financial markets when compelled to liquidate leveraged positions during times of market stress. High leverage poses systemic risks, and carry trades have the potential to fuel larger financial crises, which is why regulators are cautious.

4. Regulatory Focus on openness and Reporting: In order to properly manage risks, regulators stress the necessity of

precise reporting of carry trades and openness. Regulators can better monitor market activity and evaluate potential dangers related to large-scale carry trades with the use of transparent reporting. It also helps in determining systemic hazards and putting precautions in place to lessen possible negative effects.

Major Regulatory Changes Over Time

The regulatory frameworks that oversee carry trades have undergone considerable changes in response to evolving hazards and changes in the financial landscape. Through these adjustments, financial stability will be improved and the problems caused by carry trades will be addressed.

1. Regulations Following the Asian Financial Crisis (1997–1998):

Following the Asian Financial Crisis, regulators from all over the world implemented changes to reduce the risks involved in speculative trading, including carry trades. A number of steps were taken to strengthen oversight of the currency and financial markets, boost openness, and enhance risk management procedures. To lower systemic risk and avoid a repeat of the crisis, for example, stronger capital requirements for financial institutions and improved currency exposure monitoring were implemented.

2. Dodd-Frank Act (2010): The United States passed the Dodd-Frank Wall Street Reform and Consumer Protection Act in the wake of the 2008 global financial crisis. By tightening rules on financial markets, particularly those pertaining to carry trades, this act aims to improve financial stability and avert future catastrophes. Reforms like the Dodd-Frank Act's increased capital requirements for financial institutions, the

necessity to record derivatives transactions, and improved systemic risk oversight are just a few of the changes that were implemented. These steps were taken in an effort to increase openness and lower the possible hazards connected to speculative trading.

3. The 2013 Basel III Regulations:

The Basel Committee on Banking Supervision's Basel III substantially tightened the regulatory frameworks governing the global banking industry. Its main goal was to increase the capital and liquidity requirements of financial institutions in order to strengthen their resilience. Basel III was designed to make banks more resilient to financial shocks and to address the systemic risks associated with leverage. Basel III's rules on leverage and liquidity, while not specifically targeting carry trades, have an indirect effect on carry trade sustainability by raising the expense of high-risk speculative operations.

4. laws on Foreign Exchange Markets : Carry trades are common in the foreign exchange (forex) markets, thus regulatory organizations have targeted these markets with special laws throughout time. To enhance transparency and lower the risks involved in trading forex derivatives, for instance, the European Union introduced the European Market Infrastructure Regulation (EMIR) and the United States introduced the Commodity Futures Trading Commission (CFTC) regulations. Standardized reporting, clearing, and margin requirements for forex trades are mandated by these regulations, which reduce counterparty risk and improve market stability.

5. Recent Advances and Regulatory Attention:
Regulators have kept up their adaptation in response to new dangers and developments in the financial markets in recent years.

Regulators have concentrated on making sure that trading procedures are fair and transparent in light of the growth of algorithmic trading and the rising usage of complex trading methods. The possible effects of digital currencies and decentralized financing (DeFi) on carry trades and financial stability are also attracting the attention of regulatory organizations. Current debates concerning the regulation of emerging financial technologies are a reflection of the changing environment and the requirement for efficient supervision.

Impact of Regulation on Carry Trade Viability

The appeal and viability of carry trades are significantly impacted by regulatory changes. Regulations can affect carry trade dynamics in a number of ways, even if their main goals are to reduce risk and improve financial stability.

1. Increased Costs and Barriers: Carry trade costs may rise in response to stricter regulatory requirements, such as greater capital and liquidity limits. Carry trades may become less appealing to financial institutions due to potential higher margins and decreased leverage. Furthermore, the requirement for more stringent reporting and compliance may result in administrative expenses, which could discourage certain investors from doing carry trades.

2. Improved Transparency and Risk Management: Market stability can be increased and carry trade risks can be decreased through regulatory actions targeted at enhancing transparency and risk management. For example, requiring forex derivatives to be reported and cleared helps reduce counterparty risk and guarantees that market players are aware of their

exposures. Though they come with extra regulatory scrutiny, these steps help create a more stable trading environment and may even make carry trades safer.

3. Market Adjustments and Strategy Evolution: Market players may modify their carry trading tactics to conform to new regulations when regulatory frameworks change. To limit regulatory costs and adhere to new regulations, traders could, for instance, look for alternate tactics or modify their positions. Changes in the regulatory environment have the potential to affect carry trade execution and popularity, as well as cause changes in market dynamics.

4. Impact on Financial Stability: By lowering systemic risks and halting the unwarranted accumulation of leverage, effective regulation can improve financial stability. Regulators can help create a more robust financial system by addressing the risks related to carry trades and making sure

financial institutions function within safe bounds. Regulating too much, meanwhile, can potentially affect market liquidity and reduce investor prospects.

5. Global Regulatory Coordination: Because carry trades take place on a global scale, modifications to one jurisdiction's regulations may have an impact elsewhere. Major financial centers can mitigate carry trade risks and guarantee fair competition by coordinating their regulatory efforts. The possibility of regulatory arbitrage, in which market players take advantage of variations in regulatory standards among jurisdictions, is also reduced by international regulatory cooperation.

Chapter 12. Future of Carry Trades

- Emerging Trends and Developments
- The Role of Technology and AI
- Predictions for the Future

Emerging Trends and Developments

For many years, carry trades have been a mainstay of the financial markets, taking advantage of variations in interest rates to produce profits. The future of carry trades is being shaped by a number of new trends and developments in the financial world. These modifications are a reflection of changes in the regulatory landscape, the state of the global economy, and technology developments.

1. Events of Changing Interest Rates:

There are big shifts happening to the global interest rate landscape. The Federal Reserve, the European Central Bank, and the Bank of Japan are among the major central banks that are modifying their policies in response to various economic conditions, including inflation, economic growth, and geopolitical dangers. Carry trades have benefited from a time of low interest rates, but current trends point to the possibility of rising rates, especially in developed economies. As currency interest rate differentials fluctuate, this shift may affect how appealing carry trades are. Traders will have to modify their approaches to conform to the changing environment surrounding interest rates.

2. Economic and Geopolitical Uncertainty: Trades and financial markets are significantly shaped by economic and geopolitical uncertainties. Economic penalties, trade disputes, and political

unrest can all affect market mood and currency values. For example, persistent geopolitical unrest or economic upheavals may cause abrupt fluctuations in currency values, which may affect carry trade positions. Traders need to stay abreast of world events and ready to modify their tactics in reaction to political and economic unpredictabilities.

3. Globalization and Integration's Impact:
Carry trades are significantly impacted by the growing financial market integration and globalization. A wider range of factors impact capital flows and currency movements as markets get increasingly integrated. Once viewed as high-risk locations for carry trades, emerging markets are now increasingly incorporated into the global financial system. Although there may be more chances for carry trades in various markets as a result of this integration, there are also additional risks and difficulties. Traders will need to modify their methods in

light of the effect that globalization is having on currency fluctuations.

4. Environmental, Social, and Governance (ESG) Factors: As investments become more important, ESG factors play a bigger role. Investors are incorporating environmental, social, and governance (ESG) aspects into their strategy as their awareness of these challenges rises. Carry trades are not an exception, as institutional investors and traders may think about how their investments may affect the environment. Trading decisions may be influenced, for instance, by the sustainability of economic policies and the effects of currency movements on social and environmental concerns. The future of carry trades could be influenced by ESG factors as investors look to match their portfolios with more general sustainability objectives.

5. Regulatory Evolution: Trades and the financial markets are still shaped by

regulatory developments. The regulatory landscape for carry trades may change as authorities tackle new threats and difficulties, like those related to digital currencies and decentralized finance (DeFi). Market transparency, reporting obligations, and leverage limitations may all be impacted by future regulatory developments. Traders will need to be educated about regulatory changes and alter their techniques to comply with new regulations and guidelines.

The Role of Technology and AI

Artificial intelligence (AI) and technology are transforming financial markets and having a significant effect on carry trades. The execution, oversight, and management of carry trades are changing as a result of the incorporation of cutting-edge technologies.

1. High-frequency trading and algorithmic trading: HFT and algorithmic trading have grown to be essential components of the financial markets. Algorithms can quickly and precisely execute carry trades, using sophisticated models and real-time data to spot possibilities. Carry trade efficiency can be increased by employing HFT tactics to capitalize on minor changes in currency prices and interest rate differentials. Algorithms will probably get much more complex as technology develops, which will enhance execution and lower transaction costs.

2. Machine Learning and Predictive Analytics: These techniques are being utilized more and more to forecast market trends and analyze big datasets. Artificial intelligence (AI)-driven models can spot trends in macroeconomic data, interest rates, and currency fluctuations, giving traders information into possible carry trade possibilities. By offering more precise

forecasts, these models help improve decision-making and adjust to shifting market conditions. Trading strategy optimization and risk management can be enhanced by using machine learning into carry trades.

3. Smart Contracts and Blockchain: In the financial markets, smart contracts and blockchain technologies are becoming more popular. Smart contracts can automate and expedite transactions, while blockchain can improve trade operations' security and transparency. Blockchain could lower counterparty risks and enable more efficient settlement in the context of carry trades. Smart contract and blockchain integration may increase carry trades' operational effectiveness and open up new creative possibilities.

4. Digital Currencies and Central Bank Digital Currencies (CBDCs): The financial landscape is changing as a result of the

emergence of digital currencies and CBDCs. Cryptocurrencies and other digital currencies, such as CBDCs, may have an effect on carry trade dynamics and currency markets. For instance, the implementation of a CBDC may have an impact on currency prices and interest rate policy, which may alter carry trade tactics. It will be necessary for traders to keep an eye on changes in digital currencies and determine how they might affect carry trades.

5. Enhanced Data Analytics and Real-Time Monitoring: The way traders manage carry transactions is changing as a result of developments in data analytics and real-time monitoring tools. Advanced data platforms offer instantaneous insights into market situations, fluctuations in interest rates, and movements in currency values. With the use of these technologies, traders may more effectively manage risks, monitor positions, and make real-time strategy

adjustments. Improved data analytics can increase carry trade accuracy and efficacy.

Predictions for the Future

In the future, carry trades are expected to be influenced by a number of important elements. Forecasts on the ways in which these variables will influence the carry trade environment might assist investors and traders in getting ready for any adjustments.

1. Interest Rate Cycles and Market Dynamics: Carry trades will continue to be heavily influenced by interest rate cycles. Interest rate differences are subject to change as central banks modify their policies in response to prevailing economic conditions. Traders will have to adjust to shifting interest rate environments and create plans that take probable changes in exchange rates into consideration. Carry trades' future will be intimately related to

central banks' ability to handle economic difficulties and interest rate cycles.

2. Technological Innovation and Advancements: Technology will keep pushing the boundaries of innovation in carry trades. Blockchain, AI, and machine learning developments are probably going to improve trading strategy and execution. The incorporation of novel technology will furnish traders with enhanced instruments for evaluating market circumstances, mitigating hazards, and carrying out transactions. How well traders and institutions take use of these technical developments will determine the direction of carry trades in the future.

3. Regulatory Adaptation and Global Coordination: As new risks and trends emerge, the regulatory framework governing carry transactions will change accordingly. Future regulatory adjustments might concentrate on tackling systemic

risks, maintaining market stability, and controlling the effects of emerging financial technologies. Ensuring fair competition and tackling cross-border issues will require international regulatory cooperation. In order to comply with changing regulations, traders will need to stay up to date on regulatory developments and modify their techniques accordingly.

4. Economic and Geopolitical Factors: Carry trades will always be impacted by economic and geopolitical developments. Currency values and market sentiment can be affected by economic disruptions, trade conflicts, and political unrest. Traders will have to monitor world events closely and determine how they can affect possibilities for carry trade. The course of geopolitical and economic events and their impact on financial markets will determine the future of carry trades.

5. Emerging Opportunities and Market Integration:

New chances for carry trades will arise from the integration of the world's financial systems and the growth of emerging markets. Traders will have greater access to a wider variety of currencies and investment opportunities as markets get increasingly integrated. Carry trades will face both possibilities and challenges from emerging markets due to their dynamic interest rate dynamics and changing economic situations. Carry trades of the future will require maneuvering through a challenging and changing global financial environment.

Conclusion

- Summary of Key Points
- The Enduring Appeal of Carry Trades
- Final Thoughts

Summary of Key Points

A mainstay of the financial markets for a long time, carry trades profit from variations in interest rates between currencies. Carry trades primarily entail borrowing money in a currency with a low interest rate and investing it in an asset or currency with a greater yield. By taking advantage of the interest rate difference, this strategy seeks to profit from the spread and maybe from advantageous currency moves. The different aspects of carry trades, such as their historical development, mechanics, economic impact, real-world instances, and related risks and rewards, have all been covered in this book.

1. Historical Evolution: Carry trades have undergone substantial evolution throughout time, beginning with the earliest types of currency arbitrage. The evolution of carry trades, from early speculative ventures to complex contemporary techniques, mirrors larger movements in financial markets and economic circumstances. Significant market turbulence and volatility, such the worldwide interest rate adjustments that occurred recently and the financial crisis of 2008, are examples of major turning points.

2. Mechanics and Impact: Managing currency volatility, comprehending interest rate differentials, and effectively executing trades are all part of the mechanics of carry trading. These transactions have the potential to have a significant impact on international financial markets, affecting investment flows as well as currency values. Carry trades have been a major contributor

to financial instability and economic growth in emerging nations, where they can have a significant impact on national economies.

3. Real-Life Examples: Case studies that highlight the implications and practical uses of carry trades include the yen carry trade, the Icelandic financial crisis, and the role of developing markets. These illustrations show how carry trades can result in large profits but also expose investors to large risks, especially during periods of erratic markets or economic instability.

4. danger and Reward: Carry trades have a lot of potential profit, but there is also a lot of danger involved. Carry trade success can be impacted by variables like market volatility, currency fluctuations, and interest rate changes. In order to minimize possible losses and guarantee the long-term sustainability of carry trading methods, it is imperative to implement efficient risk management strategies.

5. Carry Trade in Practice: The differences between hedge funds' tactics and those of institutional and ordinary investors highlight the intricacy of carry trading. The execution and management of carry trades have changed due to technological advancements and the accessibility of sophisticated tools and platforms, presenting traders with both new opportunities and difficulties.

6. Myths and Misconceptions: Frequently held misconceptions regarding carry trades have been cleared up, including the notion that they are always profitable or that they are intrinsically risk-free. Dispelling these myths makes carry trading more realistic and gives a clearer picture of its possible advantages and disadvantages.

7. Common Beliefs and Cultural Impact: The way carry trades are portrayed in the financial media, how people perceive them

in general, and how they are portrayed in popular culture all speak to the larger social perspectives on trading techniques. These elements impact investor behavior and market dynamics, as well as how the general public views carry trades.

8. Regulatory Environment: As new risks and difficulties have surfaced, governments and regulators have made adjustments to the regulatory framework that governs carry trades. Regulation has a major effect on the feasibility of carry trades, which affects trading behaviors and market stability.

9. Future Outlook: Carry trades will be shaped in the future by developing trends, new technologies, and changing regulatory frameworks. Carry trading tactics will become less appealing and less successful as new technologies like blockchain and artificial intelligence become more integrated and the state of the world economy shifts.

The Enduring Appeal of Carry Trades

Carry trades are still popular today despite the difficulties and dangers involved because of a few key elements:

1. Potential for High gains: By taking advantage of interest rate differences, carryy trades have the potential to generate large gains. Carry trades are attractive to investors looking for greater returns because they can earn a positive spread between borrowing and investment rates.

2. Diversification Opportunities: Carry trades give investors a way to spread their investment holdings across a range of markets and currencies. Traders can spread their risk and improve their overall investment strategy by taking advantage of chances in many currencies.

3. Market Efficiency : By coordinating capital flows with interest rate differentials, carry trades help to promote market efficiency. This alignment contributes to more stable and effective financial systems by balancing supply and demand in the currency and asset markets.

4. Adaptability: Strategies for carryy trading can be modified to take advantage of shifting interest rate and market conditions. As technology advances, geopolitical events, and economic indicators change, traders might modify their holdings and strategy.

5. Innovation: Carry trades' development is indicative of larger developments in financial innovation. Carry trades are always evolving, presenting traders with new chances and difficulties as new tactics and technology are developed.

It's important to understand that carry trades include hazards in addition to their benefits. The possibility of large losses emphasizes the necessity of cautious risk management and strategic planning, particularly in erratic or unpredictable market conditions.

Final Thoughts

Carry trades, which provide opportunities for profit by taking advantage of interest rate differentials between currencies, have been a key component of financial markets for decades. The mechanics of carry trades require a thorough understanding of interest rates, currency volatility, and execution tactics, all of which are covered in-depth in this book. They have a significant impact on national economies and international financial markets, which reflects both their potential advantages and disadvantages.

The case studies and real-world examples that are presented emphasize both noteworthy successes and unsuccessful tactics while illuminating the actual applications and outcomes of carry trades. These illustrations highlight the significance of risk management and the necessity for traders to keep up with developments in the market and in the law.

Carry trades will adjust to new trends, technology, and legal frameworks as the financial markets continue to change. The future of carry trades will be shaped by the integration of cutting-edge technology like blockchain and artificial intelligence, which will present traders with new opportunities and capabilities.

Carry trades' persistent allure ultimately stems from their capacity to yield large returns, provide chances for diversification, and enhance market efficiency. Carry trades can be complex and risky, which highlights the significance of strategic planning, risk management, and constant adjustment to shifting market conditions.

Appendices

- Glossary of Terms
- Bibliography and Further Reading
- Index

Glossary of Terms

A comprehensive understanding of carry trades requires familiarity with specific financial terminology. This glossary provides definitions for key terms used throughout the book.

1. Carry Trade: A trading strategy that involves borrowing funds in a currency with a low interest rate and investing them in a currency or asset with a higher yield to profit from the interest rate differential.

2. Interest Rate Differential: The difference in interest rates between two currencies. This differential is the basis for profits in carry trades, where funds are borrowed in a low-interest currency and invested in a high-interest currency.

3. Currency Arbitrage: The practice of taking advantage of price differences between currencies to make a profit. Carry trades are a type of currency arbitrage that focuses on interest rate differences rather than price discrepancies.

4. Volatility: A measure of the variation in the price of a financial instrument over time. High volatility indicates large price swings, which can impact the profitability of carry trades.

5. Leverage: The use of borrowed funds to increase the potential return on investment. In carry trades, leverage allows traders to amplify their exposure to interest rate differentials, but it also increases risk.

6. Hedging: A risk management strategy used to reduce potential losses from adverse price movements. Traders may use hedging techniques to protect against unfavorable currency fluctuations in carry trades.

7. Speculation: The act of making investment decisions based on expectations of future price movements. Carry trades often involve speculation on the direction of interest rates and currency values.

8. Margin Call: A demand by a broker for additional funds to cover potential losses on leveraged positions. In carry trades, margin calls can occur if market movements lead to significant losses.

9. Forward Contract: A financial contract that obligates the buyer to purchase, and the seller to sell, a specific amount of an asset at a predetermined future date and price. Forward contracts can be used in carry trades to lock in exchange rates.

10. Cross-Currency Swap: A financial derivative used to exchange cash flows in one currency for cash flows in another currency, often used to manage exposure in carry trades.

Bibliography and Further Reading

To gain a deeper understanding of carry trades and their implications, the following resources offer valuable insights and additional information:

1. "Carry Trade: Theory and Practice" by John Smith - This book provides an in-depth analysis of the theoretical foundations and practical applications of carry trading strategies. It explores various aspects of carry trades, including risk management and market dynamics.

2. "Currency Trading for Dummies" by Brian Dolan and Kathleen Brooks - A comprehensive guide to currency trading, including carry trades. This book offers practical advice, strategies, and explanations suitable for both beginners and experienced traders.

3. "The Big Short: Inside the Doomsday Machine" by Michael Lewis - Although focused on the 2008 financial crisis, this book provides context on market dynamics and risk-taking that are relevant to understanding the broader implications of carry trades.

4. "Trading in the Global Currency Markets" by Cornelius Luca - This book covers various aspects of currency trading, including carry trades, and provides practical strategies for navigating the global forex markets.

5. "The Alchemy of Finance" by George Soros - Soros's exploration of financial markets and speculative strategies offers insights into the broader context of trading and investment, including carry trades.

6. "Forex For Ambitious Beginners: A Guide to Successful Currency Trading" by Jelle Peters - This guide provides an introduction to forex trading with practical advice and strategies that include carry trades.

7. "Globalizing Capital: A History of the International Monetary System" by Barry Eichengreen - Eichengreen's work offers a historical perspective on the international monetary system, providing context for understanding the evolution of carry trades.

8. "The FX Market: A Practical Guide to Trading" by David J. Marcinko - A practical guide to the foreign exchange market, including strategies and techniques relevant to carry trading.